Harry and Meghan

All you need to know about the new six-part

documentary (Sussexes' War on Royals)

Christopher Austin

Copyright

Table of Contents

Introduction: Harry and Meghan's Netflix All Three Episodes At a Glance

In their brand-new, explosive Netflix series, which has been called a transatlantic "TV bomb" targeted at The Firm, Meghan and Harry yesterday launched a slew of fresh jabs at the Royal Family and Britain.

A barely disguised criticism of Buckingham Palace's refusal to participate in their six-part documentary on their romance, marriage, and Megxit opens the first episode.

The privacy-conscious pair has given Netflix a wealth of images and footage from their relationship as part of their $100 million arrangement, including the moment Harry proposed in 2017 and a video of himself shooting himself in the Heathrow VIP lounge when he immigrated in March 2020.

Harry claims that he was "actually brought up" by a "second family" in Africa, where he choose to spend three-month stints in his late teens and twenties while he dealt with the loss of his mother, in the first three episodes, which would enrage his father King Charles III.

In the first episode of the couple's shocking Netflix documentary, the Duke of Sussex admits that he "had to resign" his royal responsibilities to protect Meghan Markle, likening the former Suit actress to his late mother Princess Diana.

In March 2020, the day of Megxit, when the couple chose to quit the royal family, Harry is seen recording himself in the Windsor Suite at Heathrow Airport. It will unavoidably prompt inquiries about precisely when the couple chose to collaborate with Netflix on their explosive docuseries.

Regarding Princess Michael of Kent wearing an offensive Blackamoor-style brooch in front of his wife at Buckingham Palace, Harry also mentions a "great amount of unconscious bigotry" in the Royal Family. Meghan's statement that she "wasn't truly regarded like a black lady" until she got to Britain has led to speculation that the UK is more racist and preoccupied with race than the US.

And Harry emphasized that his choice to marry Meghan sets him apart from his family because it was "from his heart" and not because she "would fit the mold," seen as a jab at his father and other senior royals, and even at his brother William.

He said that the fact that his wife is an American actress "clouded" their perception of her, but they thought it would pass quickly.

"I believe for so many family members, particularly males, there might be a temptation or an inclination to marry someone who would fit the mold instead of someone who you might be meant to be with," the Duke of Sussex remarked. the distinction between making choices based on your emotions versus your brain. And my mother undoubtedly made the majority, if not all, of her choices from her heart. And I am the son of my mother.

There will also be elements of the show that Prince William will probably find offensive, such as the choice made by his younger brother to use a portion of their mother's BBC interview with Martin Bashir, which the Prince of Wales said should never be aired again after she was tricked into participating. Harry explained the choice in his documentary, saying, "She felt obligated to speak about it. especially in the interview with Panorama. We all know, I believe, are aware that she was tricked into giving the interview, but she also talked honestly about her experiences.

As she describes meeting the Prince and Princess of Wales while wearing tattered jeans and bare feet, Meghan also criticizes the formality of the royal family. She added, when asked about what had transpired, "I was a hugger. I've always hugged people; I had no idea how strange it was to many Brits.

Additionally, she acknowledges being perplexed by the "formality" of first seeing the Queen, stating she first believed Harry was "joking" when she realized she had to bow or curtsy, and compared her first supper at Windsor to a "Medieval Times, Dinner and Tournament."

The first three episodes of the six-part docuseries, which is being released in two parts, are now accessible to view online.

Harry often compares Meghan to Princess Diana and claims that both his mother and wife were being pursued by the media in the series, which includes Meghan's tears. The "formality" of being a member of the royal family, according to Meghan, as an American, surprised her. She also says that seeing the Queen for the first time was a "shock to the system." She said that while driving, Harry had whispered to her, "You know how to curtsy, right? She said, "And I simply assumed that was a joke."

The Blackamoor-inspired brooch Princess Michael of Kent wore to a pre-Christmas function the Duchess of Sussex attended in 2017 is also discussed. She was obliged to express regret. In this family, you might sometimes be more of a problem than a solution, according to Harry. There is also a significant amount of unconscious prejudice. Unconscious prejudice is a problem, but no one is to blame for it.

"Of course now everyone is aware of my race because they made it such a big deal when I went to the UK," Meghan continues. Before that, I didn't feel like a black lady at all. Harry states that after learning she was an American actress, his family rejected her; yet, he said he knew in his "heart" he would marry her since he is his "mother's son."

In the first episode, Harry is shown in the Heathrow VIP lounge before his flight to Canada. The Duke and Duchess of Sussex start by recording themselves on the day they finished their royal responsibilities in March 2020. I don't even know where to start, sobs Meghan as she puts a towel over her head. The clip was recorded six months before their $100 million Netflix contract was finalized in September 2020, viewers noted.

The privacy-conscious couple granted the streaming behemoth exceptional access, including a vast collection of images and video from their personal life, including that of their children. Additionally, there are private messages and emails they exchanged throughout their romance. Doria, Meghan's mother, also discusses their bond in public for the first time.

The Sussexes talk about prejudice, Megxit, and their new life in California. It also states bluntly that the Royal Family refused to comment on the charges in the presentation and that it was finished in August 2022, which was before the Queen's passing.

Additionally, at the opening of the first episode, Harry may be seen recording himself at Heathrow Airport in March 2020 as he completes his last royal duties before leaving the country. I don't even know where to begin, sobs his wife as she sits on her bed in Vancouver.

The presentation began with the words "This is a first-hand account of Harry & Meghan's tale, presented using never before seen personal archive" printed in white on a black backdrop. By August 2022, every interview has been conducted. The royal family members refused to comment on the subject matter of this series.

The first episode opens with a close-up of a departures sign at an airport, with piano music playing in the background.

Harry suddenly appears on screen, and text appears stating that he is in the Windsor Suite at Heathrow Airport in March 2020.

He introduces himself while speaking into his phone's camera and says, "Hello. We are thus present on this Wednesday in March.

We recently ended our two weeks of royal engagements, which was kind of like our last push.

It's quite difficult to reflect on it now and wonder, "What on earth happened?" I mean, how did we get here? '

Images of the couple as well as media headlines and broadcasters' audio from stories about their choice to leave the royal life appear on the screen while Harry talks.

The first segment then cuts to what looks to be a phone video of Vancouver Island, Canada, shot vertically.

"H is in London and I'm here," Meghan appears with a towel wrapped around her hair and seems to be speaking into her phone's camera.

She responds, shaking her head, "I don't even know where to start."

Harry may be heard claiming that they met in London in July 2016 during the opening scene of Harry & Meghan.

After being "single for a few months," Meghan claimed she had plans to travel with friends and that a new season of Suits had been announced.

In the episode, Meghan's friend Lindsay Jill Roth is interviewed. According to Lindsay, Meghan had many vacations planned for the summer of 2016 and was just going to be free.

Pictures of Meghan with friends, including Jessica Mulroney, are shown in this section of the program.

I wanted to be alone and just have fun with girls, said Meghan.

In the documentary, a different friend named Lucy Fraser narrates: "She had planned her single-girl summer and she had a lot of plans to tour throughout Europe."

Meghan is heard saying, "I had a job." I had a good life. I knew my course. H then appeared.

He spoke about a narrative twist, to put it mildly.

Meghan was the first person Harry said he saw on a friend's Instagram.

"I was going through my feed when I came across this video of the two of them," he said. "It was like a Snapchat."

The next picture is of Meghan with the well-known dog ears filter applied.

That was the first thing, Harry remarked. Who is that, I thought. "

The buddy allegedly sent Meghan an email after that, with the lines scribbled out on the screen, saying: "Between you and I thought you would want to know this being freshly single and all." Meghan claimed this email. Prince Haz, a friend of mine, followed me after I posted about our Snapchat on Instagram, and he phoned me last night desperate to see you. Perhaps I should set you up (sic).

Who is prince Haz???? was Meghan's response, which was also spelled up on the screen.

That's the thing, Meghan stated in the first episode. Did you Google him, some people ask? ' No. That's your assignment... You think, "Let me check out what they're about in their feed," rather than what other people have to say about them.

"That was the finest barometer, in my opinion." I read through it, and it was just like gorgeous photography, with all these pictures of the landscape and the time he spent in Africa.

Then, according to Harry, they exchanged phone numbers.

He said, "We were basically in contact all the time," adding that they agreed to meet.

The Duke of Sussex claims that his family's perception of his wife because she is an American actress is "clouded."

In the second part of their Netflix documentary, Meghan admitted, "I didn't know what I was doing," about her meeting the Queen.

Harry said, "I recall my family being tremendously amazed when we first saw her; some of them didn't know what to do with themselves.

Because I believe they were taken aback. They were shocked that ginger could attract a lady who was both beautiful and intellectual.

But at first, I think that more than anything else, the fact that I was seeing an American actress made them think, "Oh, she's an American actress; this won't last."

The actress issue was, ironically, the largest issue, Meghan continued. From a British perspective, Hollywood has a strong concept of what that looks like, and it's simple for them to typecast that.

Meghan discusses her first encounter with the royal family in detail.

As she likened her first meeting with the Queen to a themed dinner at America's "Medieval Times," Meghan recently revealed what it was like to meet the Royal Family.

The Duchess of Sussex spoke about the pomp and circumstance of meeting the senior members of the Royal Family in the explosive Netflix documentary that Harry and Meghan published its first three parts on Thursday.

The 41-year-old spoke of her first "wonderful" Christmas at Sandringham, when she sat close to the late Prince Philip, Duke of Edinburgh.

And she joked that the whole event felt like an outmoded banquet at Medieval Times, a family dinner theater in the US with staged medieval-style games, sword-fighting, and jousting. She described the "intense" moment of meeting Her Majesty for the first time during lunch at the Royal Lodge in Windsor.

Meghan first interacted with a senior member of the Royal Family after she and Prince Harry made their relationship public in 2016. That person was the Queen.

As he sits with his arm around his wife, Harry informs the documentary, "She had no clue what it all consisted of." Therefore, it came as a bit of a shock to her.

Meghan said with a smile, "I mean. It's bizarre. There wasn't a huge "Now you're going to meet my granny" moment.

Until a few minutes before, I was unaware that I would be meeting her. Harry said, "Oh, my grandma is here, she's going to be there after church," as we were driving to the Royal Lodge for lunch.

We were driving when Harry said, "You know how to curtsy, right?" I can still see that moment. And I just assumed it was a joke.

How can you explain it to people, the Duke continued. How can you justify your grandmother-bowing behavior? A curtsy would also be required, particularly when speaking to an American. That's strange.

The documentary then hears Meghan say, "Now I'm beginning to realize this is a significant thing."

Americans will get this, I mean. Dinner and competition in medieval times are planned. That's how it was. I made a curtsy as if I were like... it was a pleasure to meet you, majesty.

It was quite tense. You did wonderful, Eugenie, Jack, and Fergie said when she departed. Thanks. I was acting without proper knowledge.

The documentary by Meghan and Harry on Netflix, which debuted yesterday, opens with a criticism of Buckingham Palace for declining to cooperate with the project, signaling a new front in the ongoing conflict between the Royal Family and the media.

Meghan mentions the "formality" of the royals behind closed doors in the second episode, stating she was "surprised" by this.

Because I have always hugged people, she said, "I didn't realize it is incredibly upsetting for a lot of Brits."

I believe pretty shortly I began to realize that the formality on the exterior persisted within.

There is a style of being that is forward-looking. Once the door is shut, you think, "Oh fantastic, we can now rest," and you sigh. But both sides maintain that formality. And I was surprised by it.

Recalling her first Christmas at Sandringham, Meghan said she found it 'wonderful' since she was 'with a huge family like I always dreamed.'

I very clearly recall our first Christmas at Sandringham, Meghan said. I exclaimed, "Oh my my, it's fantastic. It's just like a huge family like I always wanted," while speaking to my mother on the phone.

And she remembered a happier experience with the late-Prince Philip, who she sat next to at the royal holiday meal.

She said, "There was just this continual movement, activity, and joy. And at dinner, I was seated next to H's granddad, and I just thought it was so beautiful, saying, "We spoke about this and that." and he [Harry] was like "you had his terrible ear he couldn't hear anything you were saying" and I was like "oh... I thought it went extremely well, however.

During the early stages of their relationship, the Royal Family seemed to be "extremely pleased" with Meghan, said Prince Harry.

The Duke, however, said that his family believed his connection with the former Suits actress would never last.

In a different scene from the third episode, the Duchess of Sussex said she was unaware of what a royal walkabout was before embarking on her first one, during which the royals interact with people who had gathered on the streets.

I've never seen walkabout photos or videos. How about a walkabout? She uttered, "

I could describe to her what I had observed, as much as I knew from my own experience, Harry said. Right, the style and what a lady needed to do, how she needed to dress, and all that was the part I didn't know about.

Before Meghan's first walkabout in Nottingham, the zip on her outfit broke and needed to be safety pinned, as Meghan stated, to which Harry replied: "The entire thing was just absurd."

According to the duke, "Everyone was just so elated, pleased, and joyful." And I believe that when people saw it, they said, "Wow, what a breath of new air."

First public remarks from Doria Ragland
By unexpectedly landing a lead part in the Duke and Duchess of Sussex's upcoming Netflix series, Meghan Markle's mother demonstrates her unwavering support for the royal couple.

The 66-year-old Los Angeles resident Doria Ragland, who has remained close to the couple and her grandkids, is featured in all three of the episodes that the streaming behemoth broadcast yesterday.

Additionally, Doria takes center stage in the opening part of the second episode, declaring that she is now prepared for the world to hear her opinion on the couple's narrative and sharing how she felt when she first found out that her daughter was dating a prince.

She said she wanted to share "a little bit of my experience as her parent" with the series, including how she raised the Duchess "with a network of women."

The pair broadcast video that they started shooting in March 2020, just after their last royal engagements, in the first half of the much-awaited six-part series.

The fact that Doria talked so openly to the camera about her daughter's relationship for the first time demonstrates how close she still is to the duke and duchess.

She also says that from the moment she saw Prince Harry, she knew he was "The One" for her daughter.

Producers questioned the mother directly in front of the camera about the first time she learned about her daughter's new royal relationship in 2016.

During their phone chat, Meghan, who was playing Rachel Zane in the television series Suits at the time, allegedly murmured, "Mommy, I'm going out with Prince Harry."

I began mumbling and said, "Oh my goodness," Doria remarked.

Meghan informed her mother on that first chat that she had to keep their relationship a secret.

"From the beginning, it was extremely kind of," she said. Nobody could be sure.

Doria went on to discuss her first thoughts on her son-in-law, although she remained mum about the location or timing of their initial encounter.

He was a 6'1" tall, dashing guy with red hair who had excellent manners, she added. Simply said, he was quite pleasant. They seem to be content together.

He was The One.

Meghan Markle asserts that she was a "daddy's girl" growing up, while Harry says that she is fatherless. When Meghan Markle read her little child's poem about divorce in her new Netflix docuseries, Harry remarked, "She doesn't have a father," but Meghan argued she was a "daddy's daughter" growing up.

The Duchess of Sussex, 41, described how she spent her weekdays with her mother Doria Ragland, 66, and her weekends with her father Thomas Markle, 78, in the second episode of their new £88 million Netflix series.

Doria, a former makeup artist, and Thomas, a former cinematographer, were married in 1979 after meeting on the set of General Hospital. They later divorced when Meghan was six years old.

I do recall feeling lonely as a youngster and wanting to have more people around, Meghan added, describing herself as a "daddy's girl" as a little child.

As a result, when the Duchess was 12 years old and a student at Immaculate Heart School in Los Angeles, she was inspired to write about her experience growing up as a child of divorced parents.

One of the projects was to compose a poem about her life, and she said, "I still remember this poem today."

Meghan proceeded to recite it word by word: "Two houses, two residences, two kitchens, two phones.

I slept on two buses and I stayed at two locations. From Monday through Friday, I am always on the go.

Don't get me wrong; it's not terrible, but it frequently depresses me.

I wish to have a nuclear family, with a contented father and his devoted wife.

a fireplace with a burning log, a shaggy dog, and a picket fence.

I can't even scream or weep since it's only a dream and not real.

In this situation, things would be simpler if there were two of me.

She continued by sharing a home camera footage from 1993, during which she and her estranged father Thomas Markle went fishing.

"My dad lived alone; his two adult children had left the home," she said.

"I spent a lot of time with him and was a daddy's daughter my whole childhood."

The Duchess of Sussex issued a letter to her father requesting that he cease giving press interviews after Thomas was unable to fly from his residence in Mexico to Windsor for the couple's 2018 wedding.

Archie, 3, and Lili, 1, the 78-year-old grandfather's two grandkids, say he has never met them.

In another part of the video, Prince Harry talks about how the divorce of Princess Diana and Prince Charles affected him.

No matter what your background is, I believe most children of divorced parents have a lot in common, he said.

Being dragged from one location to another, your parents' rivalry, or spending more time in one area than you would want to and less time in another.

"There's a lot to it," I said.

When she first met Prince William and Kate Middleton, Meghan Markle said that she was "barefoot" and sporting torn jeans.

The Duchess of Sussex, 41, said that she was unaware that the "formality" persisted in private and stated she is a "hugger," which she was unaware was "jarring for certain Brits."

She acknowledged being "surprised" that there is a "forward-looking way of being and then you lock the door" in the explosive new Netflix docuseries, Harry & Meghan.

"I began to grasp that the formality on the outside carried over on the inside, that there is a forward-facing way of being, and then you shut the door and think OK, we can relax now, but that formality continues over on both sides and that was shocking to me," the speaker said.

Despite the streaming giant paying the pair a rumored $100 million (£88 million) for the fly-on-the-wall series, the couple reportedly attempted to put it back until 2023.

The royals' Netflix docuseries production crew is apparently "at strife" with them because the 'panicked' pair wants to make "such significant alterations" that they fear the film may be "shelved indefinitely," according to conflicting sources.

William and his wife Kate are not expected to watch Harry and Meghan's series firsthand, according to insiders, but King Charles and Prince William are prepared to respond swiftly and robustly' to any unfair charges made in it.

As a Netflix series depicts an emotional moment where Archie stares at a photo of his late grandma, Prince Harry claims that Meghan and Diana are "very identical."
The couple's youngster cooing over a picture of his late grandmother, Princess Diana, is one of the most heartwarming scenes fans of Harry and Meghan's new Netflix series get to witness.

Archie, now three, is shown in the heartbreaking video, which was included in the new £100 million series' inaugural episode yesterday, touching a black and white photo of Princess Diana.

In a video, Meghan is heard telling a young Archie, "That's grandmother Diana," while pointing to a portrait of Diana that hangs in their Montecito house.

In the first episode, Harry also discusses how he thought the British public swept him up after his mother's tragic death in August 1997 and how Meghan is so similar to his late mother. The pair says they are keen to preserve the late royal's legacy for their children.

The Duke of Sussex acknowledges that he has no recollections of his mother, although declaring that his upbringing was "full with laughter, filled with pleasure, and filled with adventure."

I don't have many early recollections of my mother, he said to the series' creators. It seemed almost as if I had filtered them out inwardly. However, I will never forget her mischievous chuckle.

And she often advised me to avoid being caught if I got into trouble. And inside I'll always be that snarky person.

Prince Harry repeatedly mentions his late mother in the first three episodes of the show, which began airing throughout the world at 8 a.m. today morning. He claims that the late monarch, who passed away in 1997, is "very similar" to his wife.

"So much of who Meghan is is so similar to my mother," he said in the series.

She "has this warmth about her" and "has the same compassion, sensitivity, and confidence."

The king also discussed his "secret" mourning for his mother, claiming that he had to be "stoic" and that he had to "wear two hats" following her premature death in 1997 when he was 12 years old.

"I and William were adopted as their children," he said.

But he added: "For the two of us, the expectation to see me and William out and about was incredibly challenging."

The Duke spoke out about his early apprehensions about getting married, stating he was worried that past mistakes might be repeated.

Harry said that many of his relationships didn't survive more than a few months and that he was "afraid of Meghan being pushed away by the press."

"You can see the misery of the women who married into this institution, when I got to meet M I didn't want her to be pushed away, therefore from the beginning I knew to make this work I had to keep it as quiet as possible," the speaker said, describing the early stages of the relationship.

Meghan said, "Our relationship was a gem at first; it was laid-back and pleasant."

Although Harry and Meghan showed up to their engagement party dressed as penguins, have they altered how they first met?
In their new Netflix documentary, Prince Harry and Meghan Markle have shared personal information about their courtship, including how they employed disguises and attended a secret engagement party.

The first three episodes of the six-part docuseries, of which the Duke, 38, and Duchess of Sussex, 41, who are now residing in the US with their children Archie, 3, and Lilibet, 1, revealed details of their pre-marriage lives.

As the Prince disclosed, the pair met on Instagram. Meghan described how she had planned a hot girl summer in 2016, but Harry was the 'plot twist' when they ran into one other in July.

However, according to royal admirers, the couple's episode one teaser was different from the 'how we met narrative' they had previously revealed.

The first image Prince Harry ever saw of his future bride was a photo of Meghan taken with a dog filter on Snapchat, after which they spent some time talking on FaceTime and getting to know one another.

"Meghan and I met on Instagram," Harry said. "I was going through my account when I came across this video of the two of them."

Meghan laughed and remarked, "Oh god, isn't that entire thing, it's got like dog ears," before Harry added, "That was the first thing, "I was like who is that?

His wife said, "That's absurd.

Meghan followed the Prince's Instagram account to see "what he was about" after Harry messaged their mutual acquaintance, which they told her about.

The pair had previously said they went on a blind date, with Harry telling the BBC in 2017 that it was "certainly a set-up" and "it was a blind date."

One Twitter user said that Harry and Meghan are "remarkably terrible" at remembering which falsehoods they have uttered when viewers questioned the variation.

Harry, 38, admitted to being late on their first date, which took place at 76 Dean Street in Soho, as the couple shared text messages and other information about how they met before the world knew. Harry, who is now based in Montecito, LA, with his wife and their two children, also admitted to being late on other occasions.

Additionally, Harry and Meghan discussed how they went undercover to keep their romance a secret and disclosed that during their intimate engagement party in 2017, they and their pals all donned animal onesies.

Harry is seen with a ring in his hand as he is down on one knee and surrounded by candles in never-before-seen pictures from the passionate proposal.

In the yard, near Meghan's lovely dog and a large bunch of white flowers, the prince is kneeling on a blanket.

I wanted to do it sooner, but I couldn't have done it outside of the UK since I had to get my grandmother's approval.

She said, "You never drink champagne what's the occasion," and I said, "I don't know, just had it hanging around." "I opened a bottle of champagne while she was cooking a chicken and that sort of somewhat gave the game away."

It was a magnum, Meghan said, before laughing out loud.

To pop the question to Meghan, Harry reportedly purchased 15 electric candles and put them all around their house's walled garden.

In a raw film, Meghan contacts her pal Jess in delight and whispered into the phone: 'Oh my gosh Jess. It's taking place. I was warned not to look.

Harry and Meghan, on the other hand, called their announcement of their engagement in 2017 an "orchestrated reality show," discussing how the news was spread to the globe in episode three.

Meghan asserts at the start that "we've never been permitted to speak our tale... till now before Harry agrees: 'We've never been permitted to tell our tale, that's the constant.'

Elsewhere, the pair gave glimpses of their long-distance romance with Harry and Meghan communicating through FaceTime in the early days.

One photo showed Meghan in bed with her computer, covered with selfies of her and Harry with her dog at her side. During a Facetime call, Harry could be seen looking fondly at Meghan in another private photo.

As the first three episodes of the series were published on Netflix yesterday, a sneak peek of the program included the pair in another scene remembering their first date.

'You were late,' Meghan giggled, revealing Harry continued texting her, writing: "I'm hit in traffic, I'm so sorry, I am in traffic, I am sorry".'

Meghan claimed she wondered aloud, "Is this what he does, this I'm not doing," while waiting by herself for him to arrive. Harry said, "I was panicked, I was freaking out, I was so sweating."

She questioned if he was "one of those men with so much ego that any female would wait and sit around for you for thirty minutes," as she put it. She said, "I wasn't interested in it."

But when Harry arrived, she learned that she was mistaken. I was a crimson ball of mush when I stepped in, he continued, feeling hot and sticky.

Harry was 'genuinely like so mortified you were late,' Meghan said while laughing.

Additionally, the pair uploaded a photo from their second date, which they had at Soho House.

The pair talks about keeping their romance a secret for the first several months. They post many pictures and videos from the time, including one of Prince Harry having fun with some swans.

The video, which Meghan captured, shows the couple having fun and being at ease while spending time together before their relationship was made public.

Meghan and Harry may be seen sharing a kiss in one very intimate picture of the pair from the time.

Meghan and Harry talked about their first week together in Botswana in episode one, which was another private reveal.

I had one week off from work, and it was the same week, so he asked if I wanted to go to Botswana, Meghan recalled. Let me think about it, I said, and I did.

Given that he had only seen Meghan twice before, Harry acknowledged that he was "astonished that she said yes."

We will be staying in a tent for ten days with this lady who I have only met twice and who is traveling to Botswana, he continued.

"I'm getting on a plane, and we're going to be living in the middle of a jungle. What, like, what if we don't get along, and then we're trapped in a tent in the middle of a bush?" Meghan said.

So, I arrive; this is the first time I'd seen him in a month. We are uneasy at first; should we embrace or kiss, and all I can remember is that he gave me a chicken sandwich.

Then we boarded a land cruiser and departed, Harry said. Everything seemed natural as we kissed while holding hands and held one other's faces while seated close to one another. Before the rest of the world knew, we had to get to know one another.

In the first episode of the documentary series, Lindsay Jill Roth, a friend of Meghan's, said that Meghan "had a couple of different trips planned, and she was just going to be free" in the summer of 2016.

Prince Harry confessed the first time he saw a photo of Meghan was a shot of her with a dog filter on.

Meghan said, laughing, "Oh my god, isn't that entire thing, it's got like puppy ears."

'That was the first thing, "I was thinking who is that?",' Harry added, with Meghan adding: 'That's absurd.'

Following this, Harry messaged their mutual acquaintance to contact Meghan.

Meghan said that she had anticipated an alone summer and that "H had a work life and a destiny."

Meghan remarked, "She sent me an email," as the message's contents appeared on the screen.

Being freshly single and all, I figured you would want to know about us.

Prince Haz, a friend of mine, followed me after I posted about our Snapchat on Instagram, and he phoned me yesterday night eager to meet you. The message said, "I may have to set you up."

When asked why she wanted to view the royal stream, Meghan said, "So that's the deal. "Did you Google him?" people ask.

That is, however, your homework. That, in my opinion, was the finest barometer,' she said. "You're like, "Hmm let me see what they're about in their feed, not what someone else thinks about them but what they are putting out about themselves."

Then we exchanged phone numbers. We simply kept in contact all the time, and I suggested a meeting, Harry continued.

Meghan contacted her buddy Silver Tree and said, "Silver, you're not going to believe this," according to Silver Tree. She essentially informed me that she would be going out with him.

We found it to be quite amusing. She said, "In what universe does this happen?"

Harry explained his attraction to the Hollywood star, saying, "I'm my mother's son; I make choices from my heart, not my mind."
I simply opened my heart to see what was going to happen, he continued.

Harry thought back on the "unhealthy" beginning of the romance.

Dating "became a mix of automobile cash, multi-surveillance driving, and disguises," he said, adding that this wasn't a very healthy way to begin a relationship.

But Meghan noted that when they first started dating seriously, the pair was also "relaxed and easy."

"It was laid-back and simple." We are still getting to know one another. The question "what do you like to eat, what do you like to prepare, what movies do you enjoy?" was directed to any other couple.

Princess Diana's son also said that he wasn't sure he wanted to seek a new romance because of his prior connections.

The individual and their family were hounded and had their life turned upside down by the third or fourth woman, and he stated that he wasn't sure whether he wanted this. "Every relationship that I had, for weeks or months, was splattered throughout the tabloids."

Therefore, when I finally met "M," I was scared that the media—which had pushed away so many people from me—would drive her away from me.

I was aware that keeping it a secret for as long as possible was the only way it could succeed, he said.

As the first three episodes of the program were published on Netflix yesterday, a sneak peek of the series showed the pair remembering their first date.

Meghan chuckled as she recalled Harry's repeated messages to her, saying, "I'm hit in traffic, I'm so sorry, I'm in traffic, I'm sorry."

Harry said, "I was sweating, I was frightened, and I was really upset."

Meghan said that while waiting for him to arrive alone, she found herself questioning, "Is this what he does, this I'm not doing?"

She said that she questioned if he was "one of those men with so much ego that any female would wait and sit around for you for 30 minutes."

She said, "I wasn't interested in it."

But when Harry arrived, she learned that she was mistaken.

I was a crimson ball of mush when I stepped in, he continued, feeling hot and sticky.

Harry was "genuinely like so mortified you were late," Meghan said with a smile.

In 2017, when things between them took a serious turn, the pair revealed their engagement to the public after keeping it a secret for a few weeks.

A friend recalls how Harry and Meghan invited their pals to an engagement celebration.

Everyone was dressed in animal onesies for a little engagement celebration, she claimed.

Because penguins are lifelong partners, Meghan and Harry were dressed alike in penguin onesies. They were also very lovely, she said.

The very private moments that Harry and Meghan enjoyed, including pictures from their engagement dinner and family photos.

There are many private moments that Prince Harry and Meghan Markle have chosen to make public in their Netflix docuseries.

The Duke and Duchess of Sussex, who reside in Montecito, have improved the course of their relationship from the early stages of trading dates to their marriage and parenthood.

Chapter 2: Episode One in More Detail

Face Times

The pair met on Instagram, and Prince Harry saw his future bride for the first time in a photo of her wearing a Snapchat dog filter. After that, they continued their conversation on FaceTime as they got to know one another.

In the first scene of the documentary series, Harry and Meghan may be seen communicating through FaceTime.

A picture of Meghan in bed with her computer and a wall of selfies of her and Harry with her puppy at her side was captured.

During a Facetime call, Harry could be seen looking fondly at Meghan in another private photo.

Engagement

In never-before-seen pictures from the romantic proposal, Harry recorded the guy holding a ring as he's down on one knee and surrounded by candles.

In the yard, near Meghan's lovely dog and a large bunch of white flowers, the prince is kneeling on a blanket.

I wanted to do it sooner, but I couldn't have done it outside of the UK since I had to get my grandmother's approval.

She said, "You never drink campaign what's the occasion," and I replied, "I don't know just had it hanging around." "I cracked a bottle of champagne as she was preparing a chicken and that sort of somewhat gave the game away."

Lilibet's pregnancy

On Valentine's Day in 2021, the pair shared another private photo of them in their garden with Archie along with the news that Meghan was pregnant.

Their daughter spent her first birthday in London with the Queen after being born on the first of July of last year.

Archie receives a lip kiss from Meghan.

Throughout the video, there are several clips and photographs of Meghan and her small boy playing and cuddling together, demonstrating their strong relationship.

There is, however, one especially private scene in which the Duchess picks up her son and kisses him on the lips.

The two-parent royal family can be seen hugging their kid as he lays his hands on each side of her face for a kiss.

The video, which may have been captured by Prince Harry, shows Archie wearing a sleep sack as he looks to have just woken up from a nap.

The first birthday of Archie

The Duke and Duchess of Sussex have been famously guarded about their little son, so this is one of the first pictures of Archie that admirers of the royal family have seen.

However, they revealed some images and videos of Archie, including one in which he experiences snow for the first time, in the first episode of their brand-new £100 million Netflix documentary.

Videos of him running on the beach, at their house, and the couple cuddling with the child are quite intimate.

First-time snowfall for Archie

In one endearing scene from the video, Meghan is shown rushing her kid outdoors so he can see snow as she is dressed in a large green anorak.

The pair is said to have temporarily resided on Vancouver Island at the time the footage was being shot.

They had left the UK at the time, in the fall of 2019, and were reportedly enjoying a little holiday from their royal responsibilities.

They then spent Christmas at a $14 million house on Vancouver Island in Canada.

She is heard saying, "Look at the snow! Observe the snow! '

The little child, who was wearing a vivid blue snowsuit, can be seen gazing up at his mother while being held by her.

Archie's twilight

Archie, the son of Prince Harry and Meghan Markle, is heard making a kind remark in the couple's new £88 million Netflix documentary.

The first three episodes of the Duke and Duchess of Sussex's new TV series, which debuted on the streaming platform Tuesday morning, feature their three-year-old oldest child.

In the second episode, Prince Harry may be seen walking with his kid in a location that looks to be close to their Montecito residence.

Prince Harry can be heard humming Heigh-Ho from Snow White as his three-year-old son walks in front of him.

Harry pushes Archie while carrying the bag

At home, while playing with his kid, Prince Harry was wheeling a suitcase with Archie sitting on top of it.

The Duke may also be seen pushing his small son Archie about on top of a suitcase.

They may have been residing on Vancouver Island when the video was captured.

Playing on the wooden flooring of the home seems to make Prince Harry and his kid very happy.

Riding on Prince Harry's shoulders

The small youngster is seen being carried on the shoulders of Prince Harry and his infant son Archie.

The couple, who are both wearing white t-shirts, can be seen staring at one another as they take pleasure in the bright weather.

The tiny child, who is wearing a white t-shirt, blue striped pants, and lovely little blue Croc shoes, is one of the most clearly depicted royal admirers have ever seen.

Archie and Meghan are going to the theater.

In a picture posted on the top of their 2018 Christmas card, the Duke and Duchess of Sussex displayed a spectacular playhouse constructed for their son in the yard of their residence in Montecito, California, in 2020.

Toy experts told FEMAIL that the pair might have spent up to $7,000 on the small home, which was created in the typical British manner.

According to Jamie Stanford, managing director at UK-based toy company Liberty Games, the playhouse has a "rustic British cottage" feel and "English countryside vibes" that wouldn't look out of place in the grounds of one of the British royal residences. It also has a thatched roof and split stable doors.

The playhouse resembles the Wendy home that Prince Harry's grandmother, the Queen, received from "the people of Wales" on her sixth birthday and still stands on the grounds of Windsor's Royal Lodge.

However, the playhouse was shown in a brighter light in the latest documentary when Meghan and Archie approached it while wearing similar costumes.

In the video, the mother and son pair walked together across the yard to the expensive playhouse while sporting similar cream blouses, tan pants, and brown Ugg boots.

Archie and Meghan snuggling in the vehicle

In the backseat of a vehicle, Meghan can be seen snuggling with her son Archie. Also visible is the little child curled up on his mother's lap as they travel.

Archie is seen in the automobile clutching an American flag while sporting a casual outfit of a shirt and pants.

Meghan looks to be kissing her baby son while holding onto his head.

Reading aloud to the kids

Prince Harry may be seen cuddling up to one of his kids on the couch at his $14 million residence at one point in episode two.

In the video, The Duke looks to be reading a book with a young Archie while reclined on the couch.

Pula and Guy, two of the couple's dogs, are also seen relaxing with the Prince.

Although it is unknown whether Meghan or the documentary filmmakers shot the tape, it gives a close-up view of the couple's existence at home with their kids.

Visiting Botswana

In the first episode of the interesting documentary, Meghan and Harry shared another private detail about their first date: a week they spent together in Botswana.

I had one week off from work, and it was the same week, so he asked if I wanted to go to Botswana, Meghan recalled. Let me think about it, I said, and I did.

Given that he had only seen Meghan twice before, Harry acknowledged that he was "astonished that she said yes."

We will be staying in a tent for ten days with this lady who I have only met twice and who is traveling to Botswana, he continued.

"I'm getting on a plane, and we're going to be living in the middle of a jungle. What, like, what if we don't get along, and then we're trapped in a tent in the middle of a bush?" Meghan said.

So, I arrive; this is the first time I'd seen him in a month. We are uneasy at first; should we embrace or kiss, and all I can remember is that he gave me a chicken sandwich.

Then we boarded a land cruiser and departed, Harry said. Everything seemed natural as we kissed while holding hands and held one other's faces while seated close to one another. Before the rest of the world knew, we had to get to know one another.

Meghan feeds a chicken to a newborn.

Another scene from the first episode of the show shows Meghan feeding the hens at the couple's $14 million estate while holding a baby strapped to her breast.

The infant may be seen with a lovely hat with pom-poms on top.

Although it's unclear whether the infant is Lilibet or an infant Archie, the pair has previously shared photos of Archie tending to the hens.

The little child, who is wearing trousers, a grey t-shirt, and yellow Peppa Pig Hunter wellies, is seen feeding chickens in the yard of his parent's $19 million property in Montecito, California, in the picture released during the blockbuster Oprah interview.

In a shocking interview with Oprah Winfrey, Meghan and Harry previously disclosed that they had saved chicks from a factory farm who were about to be put to death.

They reside in a hut with the inscription, "Archie's Chick Inn." Founded in 2021.

The pair discusses keeping their romance quiet for the first several months in the first episode of the Netflix drama.

They post many pictures and videos from the time, including one of Prince Harry having fun with some swans.

The video, which Meghan captured, shows the couple having fun and being at ease while spending time together before their relationship was made public.

Meghan and Harry may be seen sharing a kiss in one very intimate picture of the pair from the time.

The pair met on Instagram, and Prince Harry saw his future bride for the first time in a photo of her wearing a Snapchat dog filter. After that, they continued their conversation on FaceTime as they got to know one another.

First dates

The couple shared text messages and other information about how they met before the world knew about them. Harry, 38, who is now based in Montecito, LA with his wife and their two children, acknowledged that he was running behind schedule on their first date, which took place at 76 Dean Street in Soho.

As the first three episodes of the program were published on Netflix yesterday, a sneak peek of the series showed the pair remembering their first date.

Meghan chuckled as she recalled Harry's repeated messages to her, saying, "I'm hit in traffic, I'm so sorry, I'm in traffic, I'm sorry."

Harry said, "I was sweating, I was frightened, and I was really upset."

Meghan said that while waiting for him to arrive alone, she found herself questioning, "Is this what he does, this I'm not doing?"

She said that she questioned if he was "one of those men with so much ego that any female would wait and sit around for you for 30 minutes."

She said, "I wasn't interested in it."

But when Harry arrived, she learned that she was mistaken.

I was a red ball of the mash when I walked in, he said, feeling hot and sweaty.

Harry was "genuinely like so mortified you were late," Meghan said with a smile.

Additionally, the pair uploaded a photo from their second date, which they had at Soho House.

Halloween celebration with Jack and Eugenie

The Duchess of Sussex previously told how she and the Duke went out incognito in Halloween costumes with his cousin and her then fiancé for the last night out before their romance was disclosed on the Ellen DeGeneres program.

The pair also released many pictures from the big night out in yesterday's premiere of their new £88 million Harry & Meghan series.

Meghan and Harry can be seen squeezing in for a shot with Eugenie, Jack, and another acquaintance, Marcus, in one image.

Prince Harry and Meghan kiss each other

The duo seemed unassuming because of their similar green wellington boots, green coats, and trousers.

The ultra-glamorous Meghan, on the other hand, arrived without makeup and had her hair pulled back into a ponytail.

Although it is unknown when the photo was shot, it seems to provide a glimpse into the couple's life in Windsor.

Going to the beach covertly

The documentary reveals that in September 2020, the couple was in Big Sur, California.

While filming Prince Harry, Meghan can be heard saying, "We've gone wild," as the two giggle together.

I feel like we're doing something so dirty, she continued.

They were observed strolling to a remote beach when she said, "Oh my goodness, my love."

Meghan seemed young.

The Duchess of Sussex first appeared during her Netflix documentary series with her face uncovered and her hair wrapped in a towel.

In a Canadian-shot video, 41-year-old Meghan Markle discussed her desire to take a break from royal responsibilities while dressed casually in a denim blouse and trousers.

It was quite different from the ultra-glamorous Meghan that the public is often accustomed to seeing. Meghan is renowned for her love of expensive brands and very sentimental jewelry.

Archie, the son of Prince Harry and Meghan Markle, is featured prominently in the shocking documentary

Archie, the son of Prince Harry and Meghan Markle, has been handed the lead role in his parents' controversial Netflix documentary.

Each of the three episodes of the Duke and Duchess of Sussex's television show, which debuted on Netflix at 8 am Wednesday, included their three-year-old son.

The parents posted a heartwarming home video of their kid, who was just a few months old at the time, reaching out to touch a picture of Princess Diana that was hanging on his nursery wall in the first episode.

The video, which seems to have been shot on an iPhone inside the Frogmore Cottage residence of Prince Harry and Meghan Markle, shows Archie babbling as Meghan asks, "Who's that?" Grandma, hello! '

Meghan said, "Yeah, that's your Grandma Diana," as her infant boy reached out to touch the black-and-white photograph.

The mother and boy are shown jogging through what seems to be their Montecito home's garden together later in the episode while holding hands.

The initial episodes are peppered with fresh, never-before-seen pictures of the couple's kid, including a selfie Meghan snapped with her baby in what looks to be the Frogmore Cottage nursery and another black-and-white picture of her reading a tale to Archie as he sat on her lap.

Additionally, Meghan included a touching image during her pregnancy with Lili, who was born in June 2021.

In the phone photos, Archie is shown resting on Meghan's expanding baby tummy as she reclines on a bed in what looks to be their Montecito house.

The mother of two then kissed her son on the lips in the second episode, and it was a remarkably private moment the pair shared.

The video seems to have been recorded after the Duke and Duchess of Sussex retired from their official roles as royals in January 2020 and shows Meghan holding her infant boy in a brand-new nursery.

Then, while the touching video plays in the background, the Duchess is overheard talking about being the "product of divorce."

A short while later, Prince Harry is spotted walking with his kid at a location that looks to be close to their Montecito house.

Prince Harry can be heard humming Heigh-Ho from Snow White as his three-year-old son walks in front of him.

In other scenes, the little child is shown strolling down a trail with the family's black labrador before alerting his father that Archie is evading them.

Then a film of the father and son at their Montecito house is cut to, showing Prince Harry taking in some hummingbirds.

Prince Harry tells his kid, "We won't ever have the opportunity to get this close to hummingbirds again." Archie then queries, "Why?" while Meghan records the two of them. '

I've got a filthy foot mother since I was with you! the child cries after being told to be quiet and observe the animals.

You've got a filthy foot, honey, Meghan says to him while doing her best to contain her laughs. This is an extremely important occasion for Papa since he enjoys watching birds.

The documentary then cuts to a scene of Prince Harry reading a book to their kid while sitting on the couch.

Prince Harry remarks off-camera earlier in the episode: "My son, my daughter, and my children are mixed race, and I'm incredibly pleased about it."

"I want to be able to answer them when my kids become older and look back on this time and ask, "What did you do at this moment?" when they turn to me."

The Duke and Duchess of Sussex have been famously guarded about their little son, so this is one of the first pictures of Archie that admirers of the royal family have seen.

However, they revealed several images and videos of Archie, including one in which he experiences snow for the first time, in the first episode of their brand-new £100 million Netflix documentary.

Videos of him running on the beach, at their house, and the couple cuddling with the child are quite intimate.

In one video, the little youngster called a sunset "wonderful."

He can then be seen sprinting beside the pair as they go across the grounds of their $14 million California property.

As much as possible, Meghan and I have protected our children while simultaneously being aware of their important place in our very old family.

In one footage, Meghan talks about putting Archie and his sister Lilibet to bed while another shows a newborn Archie being moved about on a suitcase at home.

In a Netflix documentary, Prince Harry discusses how dressing up as a Nazi was the "worst mistake of my life" and how he felt "so embarrassed."
In his new Netflix documentary, Prince Harry has said that dressed as a Nazi was one of his life's "worst blunders."

The Duke of Sussex expressed regret for his faux pas from 2005 when he attended a fancy dress party wearing a costume with the famed swastika of the Nazis on his arm and the collar emblem of the German Wehrmacht.

After a photo of Harry, who was 20 at the time, wearing the outfit appeared on The Sun's front page, the story gained international attention.

Harry acknowledged his sorrow in the third episode of his and his wife Meghan Markle's new Netflix series, saying, "All I wanted to do was make things right."

In an attempt to undo the harm caused by the error, he claimed to have spoken to a Holocaust survivor and visited with the Chief Rabbi.

Jonathan Sacks was the Chief Rabbi at the time; he died away in 2020.

It was one of my worst blunders in life, the Duke of Sussex said.

I was embarrassed afterward.

"I just wanted to make it right," I said. I had a lengthy conversation with the Chief Rabbi of London, which had a significant influence on me.

"I visited Berlin and met with a survivor of the Holocaust."

"I might have moved on and disregarded it and continued to make the same errors in my life, but I learned from it."

Shortly after the photo was released, Harry apologized profusely.

I sincerely apologize if I offended or embarrassed anybody, he stated. I apologize; the outfit was a terrible decision.

When Richard Meade, an Olympic show jumper, hosted a party, the Duke of Sussex dressed in Nazi garb.

The celebration, which was arranged to honor Mr. Meade's son Harry's birthday, had "native and colonial" as its subject.

Harry donned the Afrika Korps' desert outfit, designed by General Erwin Rommel.

He had been sporting a German flag-adorned army jacket earlier in the evening.

Prince William, who was allegedly wearing a skin-tight black leotard with a leopardskin design and matching leopardskin tail and paws, had accompanied Harry when they arrived.

One visitor later said to the Daily Mail, "If this was his notion of a joke, it went down like a lead balloon."

In their new Netflix documentary, Prince Harry and Meghan Markle revealed never-before-seen images of their Halloween celebration with Princess Eugenie and Jack Brooksbank.

Before their relationship being publicly announced on the Ellen DeGeneres program, the Duchess of Sussex described how she and the Duke had one last night out together while dressing up as

Halloween characters with his cousin and her then-boyfriend.

The pair also released many pictures from the big night out in yesterday's premiere of their new £88 million Harry & Meghan series.

Meghan and Harry can be seen squeezing in for a shot with Eugenie, Jack, and another acquaintance, Marcus, in one image.

About the 2016 occasion, Meghan recalls attending a Halloween party with Prince Harry.

Meghan pulled her hat low over her face and Prince Harry was wearing a gas mask.

The duo said they intended to detonate the "fun grenade."

His cousin Eugenie, her boyfriend Jack, and my buddy Marcus were all there, according to Meghan. It was a wonderful and pure crazy joy.

Earlier this year, Meghan discussed the occasion when making an appearance on the Ellen DeGeneres show.

She described the incident to Ellen in 2016 and said: "He came to visit me in Toronto, along with his pals, his cousin Eugenie, and now her husband Jack. The four of us slipped out in Halloween costumes to just have one great night on the town before it was out in the open that we were in a relationship. We had all these pretty strange costumes on since the theme was the post-apocalypse, and we only got to go out for one last fun night.

The Duchess of Sussex and the Duke of Sussex must "not make the same errors" their parents made, according to the Duke of Sussex.

Chapter 3: Episodes Two and Three in More Detail.

EPISODE TWO

In the Harry & Meghan documentary on Netflix, the duke was shown strolling beside his American-accented son Archie.

My son, my daughter, and all of my children are mixed-race, and I'm proud of that, said Harry.

"When my children are grown up and reflect on this time, they will ask me, "What did you do at that time?"

I want to be able to respond to them.

"I believe it is our duty as human beings to do all in our power to make the world a better place for children, especially if they are brought into this world.

But equally, what's most crucial for the two of us is to avoid making the same errors that maybe our parents did.

We've just done two weeks, our last push, our list run of royal engagements, Harry explains in the movie's opening moments. It's quite difficult to reflect on it now and wonder what the heck happened. '

The Duke and Duchess of Sussex are seated next to one other on a couch in the opening shot of the first episode of the Netflix documentary Harry & Meghan.

I'm anxious, Harry may be heard saying. Why am I afraid? '

A clip of Meghan from Hello! is presented to the pair. She is asked which of Harry and his brother

William she likes in a video shot in Canada in October 2015.

In the video, she chuckles and replies, "I don't know," before the interviewer can be heard asking, "Harry?", to which Meghan responds, "Harry? Sure."

Harry, who thought the video was humorous, said that they met "less than a year" before the scene cutting back to the pair on the couch.

After apologizing to Harry, Meghan responds, "I'd pick you, of course."

OK, excellent, Harry responds before remarking, "This simply proves how little you know." Look how far we've come, too.

EPISODE THREE

The Duke of Sussex is shown talking about his ten-year military service and how it "broke" his bubble of life in the royal family.

Harry adds, after seeing a film of him speaking with US military members, "Working and living among regular people - and I completely know my life is not normal - surely has an impact on you. The bubble that I was raised in exploded inside the bubble.

The Duke of Sussex said that while raising their children, he and the Duchess of Sussex were determined "not to make the same errors our parents made."

Harry and Meghan discussed how the dissolution of their parents' marriages had influenced how they had raised their children, Archie, 3, and Lilibet, 1, in part two of their frank Netflix documentary series.

There are many things from one's youth that are carried into the present, according to Meghan. Particularly if you are a divorced person.

The two of us want to make sure that we don't make the same errors that maybe our parents did, Harry said.

"I believe that no matter your background, most children of divorced parents have a lot in common.

Being forced to move from one location to another, your parents' rivalry, staying in one place longer than you want to or staying in another place for a shorter amount of time than you want to. There are several components to it.

The Duke of Sussex has described how his parents' divorce caused him to be "drawn from one location to another."

I believe most children of divorced parents have a lot in common, no matter what your background is, he stated in the second episode of the six-part Harry & Meghan Netflix docuseries, which was published on Thursday.

The Montecito, California, in 2021 may be seen in the first episode of the Harry and Meghan documentary, which also has a dramatic crimson sky.

"Look at that," the Duchess of Sussex is heard saying. What's the best way to put it, Archie? '

And when Archie uses the word "beautiful," Meghan responds, "It's very lovely."

The Duke of Sussex is seen carrying a pram as Archie runs ahead in the family's cellphone video showing them out for a stroll.

"This is a wonderful love tale," declares Harry. The most absurd aspect is that, in my opinion, this love tale is only getting started.

She gave up all she had ever known and her freedom to join me in my world, and not long after that, I gave up everything I knew to join her in her world.

In episode three of his Netflix documentary Harry & Meghan, the Duke of Sussex said that the royal family exhibits a "great degree of unconscious prejudice."

In a 2017 event that the Duchess of Sussex attended, Princess Michael of Kent wore a brooch in the Blackamoor style, which was mentioned in the video.

In this family, there are moments when you are more a part of the issue than the solution, according to Harry. There is a significant amount of unintentional prejudice.

Unconscious prejudice is a problem, but nobody is to blame. But when it has been acknowledged or recognized by you, you must put it right.

It is instruction. It's consciousness. Everyone is always working on it, including myself.

The Duke and Duchess of Sussex discussed how their relationship survived the heightened media scrutiny in episode two of Harry & Meghan.

When all of that began occurring, Meghan said, "my friends and the people I love and care about were like, 'Is he worth this? For instance, we are aware of your happiness and your affection for him. Is this even worth it? Take a look at what is occurring in your life.

We just made every effort to support one another. We had to keep in touch. If we hadn't been, we wouldn't have survived.

I don't know how we did it, but we did it, Harry remarked. We spent most of the time across the Atlantic. I tried to see her when she was working in Canada, but she came over here to see me much more often.

As Meghan detailed arriving in the UK, being hounded, and retreating to Kensington Palace until she departed, text conversations between the pair planning visits back and forth to see one other were shown on Netflix.

Harry recalled: "Dating turned into this mix of vehicle chases, anti-surveillance driving, and disguises. It's not a healthy way to start a relationship, but we always approached it with as much humor as we could.

"Whenever we saw one other, we simply gave each other a huge embrace and tried to live as normally as we could."

The Duchess of Sussex said that she was surprised by the "formality" of becoming a member of the royal family.

In episode two, the Duke of Sussex referred to Meghan's first encounter with the Queen as a "shock to the system."

Meghan initially met a senior member of the family, my grandmother, according to Harry. It was kind of a shock to her system since she had no concept of what it all included.

There wasn't a huge "Now you're going to meet my grandma" moment, said Meghan. Before meeting her, I was unaware that I would.

"Oh, my grandmother's here; we're going to see her after church," he said as we were on our route to Royal Lodge for lunch. I recall we were in the vehicle as we approached and he said, "You know how to curtsy, right?

And I only assumed it to be a joke.

How do you explain it to folks, Harry asked. How can you justify your grandmother-bowing behavior? Additionally, you must bow. to an American in particular. That's strange.

I'm beginning to see that this is a major thing, Meghan continued. Americans will comprehend this, after all. We have meals, a tournament, and medieval times. That is how it was.

Meghan inquires, "Do we have that pap on a scooter again - the same guy?" to which the bodyguard responds, "Yes," as the pair finds themselves delayed in traffic congestion and realize they are being followed by a photographer on a scooter.

The Duchess of Sussex reminisced on the days leading up to their May 2018 wedding in episode three of Harry & Meghan, alleging that "salacious" articles were "seeded" by the media.

We were playing whack-a-mole, she said. It was like, "Wait, another one sprang up; wait, pause, another one," every single day. Constant. To produce and plant the most obscene tales they could, they were digging through the woodwork and removing individuals. The situation then became ominous.

The program then includes news articles from the UK's Mirror, Australia's New Idea, and the US's National Enquirer discussing their increased security when a mail containing white powder was delivered, leading to an anthrax fear.

It was immediately after those terrible incidents, so there is a lot of worry during the wedding, Meghan continues. It was quite frightful. They discussed acquiring snipers.

She said that she was "simply turtling" "behind the scenes."

The Duke of Sussex said in the first episode of Harry & Meghan that a friend advised them to capture this specific time in their life.

A buddy of ours advised that we record our experiences at this time, he added.

It looked like a very rational plan in light of the widespread false information, particularly about us and the departure.

When asked whether this is her first video, Meghan seems to say: "I don't know" while speaking into her phone camera. We have discussed it. We continue to discuss it because we are aware that while it may not make sense today, it will in the future.

She is heard saying in an interview clip, "We've been pretty concerned about safeguarding our kids as best we can and also recognizing the position that they have in this incredibly historical family."

The Duke of Sussex claims that his family's perception of his wife because she is an American actress is "clouded."

In the second part of their Netflix documentary, Meghan admitted, "I didn't know what I was doing," about her meeting the Queen.

The documentary's opening titles show a video of Harry and Meghan riding in their carriage on their wedding day as well as a picture of the late Queen riding in a carriage.

In addition, they show the King receiving the title of Prince of Wales during his investiture, Harry as a young boy with Diana, Princess of Wales, and Meghan looking into a sea of Union flags.

There are images of Harry as a young man, the couple gazing fondly at one another, the Duke and Duchess of Sussex presenting their baby, Archie, to the media, Harry as a child, and what seem to be photos of the couple enjoying fun taken in a photo booth.

Harry's voice can be heard stating, "My responsibility is to keep my family safe," as the couple is seen presenting their son Archie to the media. I'm typically afraid for the safety of my family because I was born into this position, everything that goes with it, and the degree of hatred that has been incited over the past three years, particularly towards my wife and my kid.

Then, with a towel in her hair, Meghan can be seen once again stating, "I just really want to get to the other side of all this."

She pauses and sits still before saying, visibly moved, "I don't know what to say anymore."

Harry says: "So like duty and service and I feel as if being part of this family it is my job to discover this exploitation and bribery that occurs inside our media" at the start of the first episode.

Sadly, Meghan claims, they are harming us because we are standing up for something.

Harry explains, "This isn't only about our narrative," as the piano music carries on. We have never been a little part of this.

Nobody is fully aware of the truth. The whole truth is known to us. The institution is well aware of this reality. And since they were privy to it, the media is aware of the whole truth.

And I believe that anybody else in my shoes would have acted precisely the same way.

When Harry adds, "And then the zip breaks," Meghan admits she worried about her clothing and if her earrings were made by a British designer before making sure to remove the tags. Everything about it was absurd.

During the second Harry & Meghan episode, Meghan's mother Doria Ragland discussed how the media had covered her daughter's upbringing and mentioned how they would photograph impoverished areas of Los Angeles.

They would take images of various areas like, let's say, Skid Row and claim that I lived there and that was where she was from, Ms. Ragland said in the Netflix documentary.

It was awful, Meghan said.

But I kept holding the line. Stay silent.

According to the Duke of Sussex, when the royal family questioned media headlines about the Duchess of Sussex, they questioned why she should be "protected."

The six-part Netflix documentary series Harry & Meghan's second episode included him saying: "The Palace's instruction was don't say anything."

"However, what people need to realize is that a large portion of the family had also gone through what she was going through.

The family members believed that if their wife had to go through it, why should their girlfriend be treated any differently? As a result, it was almost like a rite of passage. Why should you be treated differently? Why does she need to be protected? "

I said, "The aspect of the race here makes a difference."

Following the release of two trailers in which the pair claimed they were not protected by royal authorities and that aides intentionally 'fabricated rumors' about them as part of a 'dirty game,' Buckingham Palace prepared for the worst.

Prince William and King Charles are reportedly prepared to reply to the series if required.

Prince William and King Charles are reportedly prepared to respond swiftly and robustly' to any unfair charges made in Harry and Meghan's forthcoming Netflix series, although insiders suggest William and his wife Kate are unlikely to see it personally.

Members of the now-defunct Sussex family are reportedly "seething with wrath" after seeing the teasers for the six-part series.

According to reports, King Charles and Prince William are unsure of how they will react to the play (seen above with the Queen Consort and the Princess of Wales).

The Royal Family feels the series will be short on fresh disclosures.

According to a source who spoke to The Mirror, "Harry and Meghan are making a lot of noise, and there isn't much more to say."

However, preparations are being prepared for any scenario, particularly if false allegations are leveled.

The royals are hesitant to fight each other tooth and nail over the series, a source allegedly said to The Sun.

They declared: "It is only appropriate that incorrect elements get rectified.

There are several obvious mistakes and misrepresentations in the trailers already, which is not encouraging for the whole series. However, the strategy is to "remain quiet and continue."

The complete series is scheduled to be published next Thursday, but sources told the newspaper they are not expected to comment until then.

The King and Prince of Wales are said to have instructed aides to provide a "quick and forceful" reaction if necessary.

You can be sure that if there is a need to reply to anything in the forthcoming series, it will be done so quickly and forcefully.

It's believed that Netflix granted senior royals a right to reply so they could address any accusations made in the show.

However, Kensington Palace and Buckingham Palace both deny having received such a proposal.

Meanwhile, Harry and Meghan promised that it is just the "beginning" and have previously mentioned, "sweeping down barriers of tyranny."